THE

GHOSTLY TALES

OF

MARTHA'S
VINEYARD

Published by Arcadia Children's Books
A Division of Arcadia Publishing
Charleston, SC
www.arcadiapublishing.com

Spooky America is a trademark of Arcadia Publishing, Inc.

First published 2023

Manufactured in the United States

Images used courtesy of Shutterstock.com.

ISBN 978-1-4671-9730-4

Library of Congress Control Number: 2023931842

Notice: The information in this book is true and complete to the best of our knowledge.
It is offered without guarantee on the part of the author or Arcadia Publishing. The
author and Arcadia Publishing disclaim all liability in connection with the use of
this book.

Spooky America

THE GHOSTLY TALES OF

MARTHA'S VINEYARD

ANNA LARDINOIS

Adapted from *Ghosts of Martha's Vineyard* by Thomas Dresser

arcadia
CHILDREN'S BOOKS

MASSACHUSETTS

ATLANTIC OCEAN

CT   RI

MARTHA'S VINEYARD

TABLE OF CONTENTS & MAP KEY

Welcome to Spooky Martha's Vineyard!

Have you ever been to Martha's Vineyard? It's an island six miles off the coast of Cape Cod, Massachusetts, where lots of people love to spend their summers. The Vineyard is known for many things. Beautiful beaches and stunning cliffs. Charming inns and fancy shops. Salt marsh creeks and elegant seaside mansions. There are nature trails and wildlife sanctuaries where you can hike, explore, and paddle to your heart's content. And when you get hungry from all that exploring, you'll find plenty of yummy things to eat, like buttery lobster rolls and quahog chowder. (Or, as the locals say, "chowdah.")

BUT. There is something *else* the Vineyard is famous for.

Something . . . spooky.

(p.s. Before we go any further, you may want to grab your flashlight.)

Got it? Good. Because you guessed it—Martha's Vineyard is full of GHOSTS! That's right. Though this charming island destination may look as pretty as a postcard, below the surface, you'll find *hundreds* of haunted tales. Which isn't all that surprising, since many of the Vineyard's buildings and homes date back centuries—even as far as the 1600s!

With places that old and mysterious, there are bound to be spirits or supernatural forces lingering. Like Helen, a spirit who is still waiting for her husband to return from sea (and she's been waiting a loooong time). Or the inn where a man happened upon a group of British redcoats enjoying a lively party. Or the Tisbury School, which just so happens to be haunted!

The island's history goes way back, beginning with the Wampanoag, the first known people to live on Martha's Vineyard. For over ten thousand years, the Wampanoag People inhabited the area, their culture and economy centered around fishing, farming, and whaling. Then, in 1642, the first European settlement was established on the island. Settlement founder Thomas Mayhew named it Great Harbor. Today, it is known as Edgartown.

When the Europeans arrived, an estimated three thousand Wampanoag lived on the island. Within one hundred years, however, due largely to the spread of new diseases introduced by settlers, only a few hundred of the island's original residents remained. Though many died during this time, some people believe their spirits live on, still haunting Martha's Vineyard to this day.

But that is only one chapter of the island's spooky story. Despite being relatively small (Martha's Vineyard is just twenty miles long), the island has played an important part in American history.

When the American Revolutionary War started in 1775, the isolated island outpost was neutral in the conflict. (That means it did not take sides.) But when the British Royal Navy arrived on the island's shore, their behavior made the residents reconsider their stance in the conflict between the American colonies and King George III. British soldiers stole sheep, food, and weapons from the island's residents and invaded their homes. Soon, Vineyard patriots banded together to protect their homeland from

the British redcoats. (And some of those redcoats apparently never left!)

The island also played a significant role in the boom of the whaling industry in the early 1800s. Whales provided valuable oil and other resources that people needed. Successful whalers became very rich. At one time, the world's largest whale-oil candle factory in the world was on Martha's Vineyard. However, when petroleum was discovered, people no longer needed whale blubber to light their lamps, and the whaling industry became a less important part of the economy. Could some of the Vineyard's odd occurrences be the ghosts of those whaling captains, longing for their old maritime adventures?

Today, the island is best known as an East Coast tourist destination. At last count, there are over twenty thousand people who live on the island all year. But in the summer, the population of Martha's Vineyard soars to an estimated two hundred thousand people! Visitors travel to the island to enjoy the sandy beaches and historic lighthouses, and to gaze at the beautiful Aquinnah Cliffs. (Is that the wind whistling . . . or could it be the cries of a heartbroken woman who threw herself from the cliffs and vanished beneath the waves?)

With so much history—and a vibrant spirit all its own—it is not surprising that the island is brimming with paranormal activity. So whether you are in Martha's Vineyard for a summer holiday, or you live

there year-round, chances are good that you have your own spooktacular tales to share.

Read on to meet some of the island's best-known (and well-hidden) ghosts. But should you ever decide to visit this beautiful and charming place, be warned: Like the ghosts of Martha's Vineyard . . . you may *never* want to leave.

North Water Street, Edgartown

Strange Happenings at the Kelley House

The Kelley House has been welcoming visitors since 1742 (almost three hundred years!). The historic hotel, located in the heart of Edgartown, is home to a popular restaurant, The Newes From America, which is, without a doubt, *haunted*.

The employees of the restaurant have witnessed many hair-raising, unexplained events over the years. Perhaps the most shocking was when a group of people saw wine glasses sailing through the air, seemingly on their own!

The shaken employees still talk about the night when two wine glasses that were on a shelf behind the bar suddenly flew through the air. The glasses traveled more than eight feet before shattering on the floor in front of the bar.

The employees ran over to investigate what happened, but they could find no explanation. The shelf that held the glasses wasn't loose. There was no one behind the bar, so the glasses weren't accidentally dropped or thrown. How did those glasses soar eight feet through the air?

Many of those same employees remember another time when an object moved without explanation. This time it was a Christmas ornament with a life of its own.

The restaurant workers recall seeing a Christmas ornament fall from a wreath hanging in the restaurant. The colored glass globe fell to the floor, then slowly rolled from the location it landed. The ornament did not break.

Before anyone could pick it

up off the floor, it bounced! All by itself! And then the ornament rolled in the opposite direction! A waitress who was there said, "It flew across the room like it was shot!" Everyone who saw the decoration's strange movements was baffled. How could it move like that without anyone touching it?

It is more than just moving objects that have people convinced the Kelley House's restaurant is haunted. Lights in the dining room are known to turn on and off without any earthly intervention. Those who have experienced this unexplained phenomenon investigated and found that the lightbulbs were in working order and were tightly screwed into the light sockets. And there was nothing wrong with the light switches, either. Could an otherworldly being have caused these strange happenings?

But the odd occurrences don't stop there. It seems that the fireplace in the restaurant has also been the source of unexplained events.

On cold days, employees often build a fire inside the restaurant's brick fireplace. Diners enjoy the cozy warmth from the fire during the dinner hour. Late in the evening, employees stop adding logs so the fire goes out by the time the restaurant is closed for the night.

On more than one occasion, however, employees have observed the glow of dying embers in the fireplace suddenly roar back to life. The flames burn brightly, as if a new log has been added to the fire, yet no one is near the fire at all! Well, no *living* person, at least.

The explanation for all these strange happenings? No one knows for certain, but it might have something to do with Helen.

Helen is a ghost who resides in Room 307 of the hotel. Her real name is unknown, but she is believed to be the wife of a sea captain who never returned from his final voyage on the Atlantic.

This spirit is only active in winter. She has been spotted lingering near the fireplace in the restaurant. Many believe the ghostly lady is responsible for lights turning on and off, as well as the occasional object moving seemingly on its own.

Those familiar with the ghost claimed to have heard the footsteps of the long-dead woman. They report that the sound of footsteps will suddenly stop, just as an empty chair moves slightly—as if the unseen Helen has walked up to the chair and sat.

Robyn, a longtime employee of the Kelley House, has a special relationship with the ghost. She has even seen Helen standing by the fireplace, wearing a dress with a "blueish glow."

Robyn remembers a time when another employee put brass candlesticks on the mantle of the restaurant fireplace. Looking at the candlesticks, Robyn knew Helen would not be happy to see them there. Robyn told the other employee Helen was not going to like where the candlesticks had been placed. As soon as the words were out of Robyn's mouth, the candlesticks fell off the mantle and onto the floor.

It is not surprising that Robyn knows the ghostly Helen so well. After all, the pair spend a great deal of time together. "I can feel her," Robyn said. "I sit down with a cup of coffee, and I think she likes the companionship."

While Helen seems to be a very active entity, all the employees agree she is a friendly ghost who would never harm the living.

But she is not the only ghost at the Kelley House. Believe it or not, Helen is just one of a number of spirits that still linger within these walls.

Another ghost people have observed in the building is that of a young boy. The spirit makes himself known by bouncing a ball throughout the hotel. The rhythmic thud of the rubber ball hitting the floor can often be heard coming from unoccupied rooms and echoing in empty hallways. Little is known about the ghostly child, but a few people have caught glimpses of him.

Better known is the apparition of a bald man

who appeared in the room of a hotel employee named Esther.

Esther was relaxing in her room one evening when the man walked through the door. He seemed not to see her there, and walked past her into the bathroom. Within moments, Esther heard the shower turn on. She patiently waited as the ghostly man completed his shower.

When the man left, the stunned Esther went into the bathroom, where she found sand on the floor. She was puzzled. How could a ghost leave traces of sand behind him?

After investigating, she learned the unexpected visitor was the ghost of a sailor who had stayed at the Kelley House many, many years ago, when he was still among the living. He frequently returns to the hotel to clean himself up, just like he did when he was alive.

People have reported seeing the apparition of a man appear near the front door of the restaurant.

Could this also be the ghost of the showering sailor?

All this activity makes the hotel a popular place for ghost hunters. In the past, ghost hunters have focused on the adjoining rooms on the third floor numbered 305 and 307. Paranormal investigators have sensed spirits in the room and even caught the scent of the perfume worn by one of the unseen entities.

Not surprisingly, it is not just the hotel and restaurant at the Kelley House that are haunted. The small cottages on the property also experience paranormal happenings. One guest took to social media to warn others after spending two spooky nights in one of the cottages.

Stephanie, the terrified guest, was roused from sleep both nights of her stay by otherworldly activity. At four in the morning, Stephanie heard the sounds of furniture being moved. While her friend slept through the commotion, Stephanie listened to the rumble of a chair being dragged across the floor in the empty room above. Her heart pounded in terror as she heard the chair move over and over again.

The next morning, an exhausted and still frightened Stephanie stepped into the Newes From America restaurant and asked the bartender if the Kelley House was haunted.

"Of course! Everything on this island is haunted," he said.

And then he proceeded to tell her about Helen, the showering sailor, and all the others who have chosen to spend the afterlife in the Kelley House.

Rest assured, these spirits have yet to check out of the historic inn. A visit to the Kelley House is all it takes to begin your ghostly adventure.

If you do encounter Helen, or any of her otherworldly friends, don't say you weren't warned!

19

CHAPTER 2

Spine-tingling Tales from Tisbury School

Would you attend a haunted school? Students enrolled at Tisbury School do!

Every student, from kindergarten all the way to eighth grade, knows the school is haunted. Kids call the spooky specter Scottie, but that might not be the right name. After all, some locals say there might be more than one ghost roaming the halls of this school.

It all began in the summer of 1929, when the Tisbury School was being built.

A man named Thane Cottrell was in charge of

the construction. He hired his twenty-one-year-old brother, Herbert, to work on his construction crew.

On July 17, tragedy struck. The brothers were building the school when a summer storm blew into town. Thane and Herbert ran into the building to secure it from the storm's heavy winds and rain. While the men were in the building, Herbert lost his balance and fell backward through an opening in the floor. Herbert plunged fifty feet before crashing onto the basement floor of the building. He died almost instantly.

Even though Herbert had died on the construction site, work on the school continued. Before long, the building was completed, and the school opened. Students and teachers filled the classrooms, but they were not alone. Lights turned on and off by themselves. Chairs and desks seemed to move mysteriously. Those who witnessed the odd occurrences believed there was a very good explanation: Herbert's spirit had remained at Tisbury.

A former student named Bonnie Bassett said, "If you were around the school at midnight, you would see the ghost or hear him screaming!"

Some of the more skeptical locals say the stories were made up to scare kids from sneaking into the school late at night. But Bonnie isn't the only one who thinks there is something supernatural happening inside Tisbury School.

Richie Smith worked at Tisbury School for years. He had a very strange experience inside the building. Late one summer evening, Richie was alone in the school, painting his third-floor office. When he began to paint the wall behind his office door, he suddenly felt a chill run through him. An otherworldly sensation, like he was not alone in the room.

As he moved behind the open door, his body began to tingle. Then, without warning, the door started to push against Richie. He described the feeling of the door hitting his back as "a forceful push."

The door nudged into him more than once.

Spooked by what was happening, Richie cried out to the ghost, "Hey, I'm just trying to make your school nicer!"

Former custodian, Glenn Maciel, is another who believes Herbert might not be the only ghost that still walks the halls of Tisbury School.

Early one morning, before sunrise, Glenn and his dog Max made their way to the school. When the pair entered the building, Max froze. The dog began to whimper and would not move.

Glenn looked down the hallway to see what had upset his dog. To his amazement, he saw an apparition! When he took a second look at the ghostly figure, he realized it looked familiar. It was his former co-worker, Scottie!

When Scottie was among the living, he worked as a custodian for the school during the 1940s and 1950s. It seems in his afterlife, Scottie was still showing up for work!

Glenn is convinced he saw Scottie. This ghost made his presence known throughout the building.

People claim Scottie spent many years lingering in the closet of Janet Stiller's third floor classroom. Others say the ghostly figure was known to sweep the hallways of the school.

However, it seems as if this busy ghost may have disappeared. In 1995, the school completed an addition to the building. After that, people no longer saw Scottie. But . . . is he really gone? Might he be quietly watching as students work on multiplication tables? Or lingering nearby when they eat lunch? Nobody knows for sure, just like nobody knows who will be the next lucky (or unlucky, depending how you feel about ghosts) student to catch a glimpse of this restless spirit.

What we do know is—whether it's Herbert Cottrell or Scottie behind the hauntings—there is almost *certainly* something eerie (and maybe even spine-tingling) going on at the Tisbury School.

A Specter in the Slammer

When you imagine what a jail looks like, you probably don't picture anything like the Dukes County House of Correction on Main Street in Edgartown. You might imagine high fences drenched in barbed wire, or heavy bars over the windows. The jail on Martha's Vineyard looks nothing like that.

Instead, the historic white wooden structure with picturesque black shutters looks more like a family home than a place where prisoners are held. Some visitors might even call this county jail . . . *charming*.

You can't see the jail cells, or anything else jail-like, from the sidewalk, but rest assured, they are there. The walls of the jail cells are made of eighteen-inch-thick granite (a type of stone that is known for being very hard and resistant to damage). Which means it would be almost *impossible* for anyone to try to escape by tunneling through the walls—at least not without some seriously noisy equipment. On top of that, thick steel bars cover the windows of the cells.

Built in 1873, this historic building has many more interesting details. And perhaps the most interesting of all is that the Dukes County House of Corrections is haunted! Some people might not believe there could be a ghost in the county jail, but there is plenty of evidence that a paranormal presence is in the building. Officers working the night shift report hearing footsteps coming from the upper levels of the building. Sometimes the sounds come from the hallways. Other times, footsteps can be heard on the wooden staircase. This always occurs late at night, long after the prisoners, who are locked in their cells, should be fast asleep.

On these nights, the officers sit at their desks, waiting, listening, and watching. But though they hear the footsteps coming closer and closer, no one ever enters the room. At least . . . no one the officers can see. Sometimes, they will even get up from their desks to poke their heads into the hallway or glance up the stairs to see who is there.

But no one ever is.

Each and every time they check, the hallways and staircases are *empty*.

One night, the officers heard so many footsteps, they were certain a prisoner had escaped. After a check of the jail, however, they found everyone securely in their cells. They searched the building from top to bottom but could find no one. In the end, they gave up the search, assuming the ghost was just having an exceptionally active night.

But unexplained footsteps aren't the only reason officers believe the Dukes County Jail is haunted. The otherworldly spirit has also been known to turn on the kitchen sink faucet and switch lights in the building on and off. Sometimes, the spirit finds even more creative (and much noisier) ways to get attention.

Officers have reported hearing the loud clack of typewriter keys struck by unseen fingertips coming from seemingly empty rooms—tapping away late into the night. They have observed radios being switched on by an unseen hand, filling vacant rooms with the sound of staticky music.

But the most chilling evidence of paranormal activity was caught on security camera. While reviewing security footage taken in the dayroom (a secure common area where prisoners can talk or watch television), officers caught a glimpse of something that sent shivers up their spines.

The camera captured a blurry figure in the room. The officers could not make out any details of what they caught on film, but the shapeless figure can clearly be seen slowly making its way across the room. What was it the officers saw? To this day, none of them are certain—but whatever it was, it was *not* human.

With this many otherworldly occurrences in the building, the question isn't *if* the jail is haunted. The question is *who* is haunting the Dukes County House of Correction.

No one really knows. Some who have experienced the hauntings for themselves think the spirit is that of former jail warden Fred Worden, still reporting for duty long after leaving this world.

But most are convinced the ghost is a former prisoner named Joe who died in the jail in 1950. That's why many around Edgartown simply know this ghost as "Old Joe."

What do you think? Is the jail truly haunted? And if so, is it a former warden still making his rounds? Or could it be a former inmate keeping an eye on the place?

Or maybe, it's both . . .

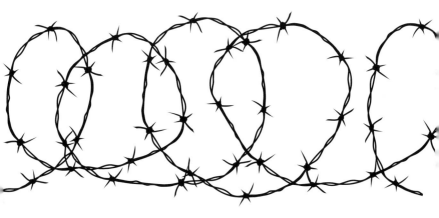

Menemsha Harbor, Chilmark

CHAPTER
4

Ghost Without a Home

Where do ghosts go when the house they haunt is destroyed?

This is a question Chilmark residents are still asking themselves after a reportedly haunted house built in 1735 was torn down.

The house played an important role in the island's history. In 1778, during the American Revolutionary War, the British used the house as its headquarters during Grey's Raid. The raid is considered one of the darkest days in Martha's Vineyard history. On

September 11, 1778, British Major General Charles Grey stormed the island with nearly forty ships and almost four thousand troops.

The British soldiers robbed the islanders, forcing them to surrender 10,574 sheep, 315 cattle, 229 guns, and countless bales of hay.

But Grey and his men were not satisfied. They began searching the homes of the islanders to find even more valuables to seize.

When the British soldiers took over the Chilmark house, they searched every room for weapons and gunpowder. They found nothing, but that wasn't because the house did not have what the men were looking for.

 Seated on a chair by the fire, a brave young girl watched quietly as the soldiers raided her family's home. While the men searched every nook and cranny, the girl smoothed her hands over her long, full skirts, which concealed the chair

she sat upon. But she was not actually sitting on a chair. Instead, the girl was perched atop a barrel of gunpowder!

The soldiers never found it.

Maybe it was this very show of defiance that invited paranormal activity into the Chilmark home.

Hundreds of years later, modern-day residents of the home experienced many strange things. Inside the house, radios would turn themselves on and fill empty rooms with music. In the kitchen, a blender was known to turn on without human intervention. This was truly unexplainable, since it happened while the appliance was unplugged!

A clock in the kitchen would often startle residents of the house. The clock did not have any batteries but somehow still managed to tick.

If those eerie occurrences weren't enough, residents reported hearing footsteps from unseen entities echo in empty hallways. Dogs who entered the house would growl while looking at the attic.

The upper floor was searched countless times, but no one was ever found lurking among the storage boxes and old trunks.

At least, no one among the living.

It seems clear that this home was haunted. So, what happened to the ghosts who inhabited that

house when the owners tore it down? Did they remain on the property, quietly waiting until a new house was built on the land, before moving back in? Or did they silently slip into nearby homes and join an unsuspecting family?

Perhaps they still wander the seaside streets of Chilmark, watching and waiting for someone to follow home?

What do you think? Where do ghosts go when the homes they haunt are destroyed?

CHAPTER 5

The Luce House

Karen Coffey knows ghosts. And she should. After all, she has been communicating with them her entire life.

Karen was born with psychic abilities. She feels connected to the spiritual world and has studied with famous paranormal researchers. Her abilities allow her to see and sense things that most people can't.

Karen has lived in many haunted houses over

the years. When she moved into the Luce House in Vineyard Haven, the spirits in the home introduced themselves to her almost immediately.

On the very first night Karen spent in the home, she had her first spooky encounter. In the middle of the night, without warning, a tall, ghostly woman appeared at the foot of her bed. The woman proudly held her chin high in the air. She looked almost regal.

Fortunately, the apparition did not want to scare Karen. Instead, the specter simply asked her to take good care of the home. That was just the first of many paranormal occurrences that happened while Karen lived in the house.

In 1990, Karen gave birth to a son. When he was a young boy, Karen often heard him chattering away. She assumed her son was talking to himself or the television.

One day, however, she listened to her son a bit more closely and was surprised. Instead of the jabber of a child practicing words, she heard what sounded like a conversation. Well, at least *half* of a conversation. She could hear that her son was speaking to someone, but she did not hear any responses.

It did not take Karen long to discover that her son was chatting with the spirit of Mikayla Luce. Mikayla was a granddaughter of Jonathon Luce, a man who used to live in the home. Young Mikayla died in a tragic accident at the Luce House.

Mikayla was on the staircase when she slipped over the banister. The girl fell down the stairs and broke her neck. She later died.

Apparently, many years later, Mikayla had found a new playmate in Karen's son.

The young boy and the ghostly girl would meet in the front hallway of the Luce House. The pair talked with each other for years.

They may even have shared the boy's toys.

Karen recalled a time when a girl she knew was

riding her bike past the Tisbury Village Cemetery. As she pedaled along the street, the girl noticed a red ball in the cemetery. She knew the ball belonged to Karen's son. The girl told Karen where the red ball could be found. When Karen went to retrieve it, she found the ball in the graveyard, just where the girl had said it would be. But when Karen looked closer, she realized something astonishing.

The red ball was sitting directly on top of the grave of Mikayla Luce!

Did the little girl often borrow toys from the boy who lived in the house where she died? If so, how did

she get the toys to and from the cemetery where her body had been laid to rest?

Karen never found out the answer. But deep down, she always felt sorry for the little girl. After all, it must get lonely for Mikayla. Her playmates would always grow up, but she would forever stay a little girl.

I wonder if there are children living in the Luce House today. If so, do you think they share their toys with the ghostly girl?

Would *you* play with a lonely ghost?

CHAPTER 6

The Haunts of Humphrey House

If you believe the rumors (and there are plenty of people who do), the old Humphrey House in West Tisbury is haunted.

If that name sounds familiar to you, it is because the family is well known for its bakery. For generations, the Humphrey family has been baking tasty treats for the whole island to enjoy.

The Humphrey House is a sprawling three-story clapboard house built in 1875. It is located across from Priester's Pond. For many years, there was a rocking chair inside the home.

That rocking chair became legendary.

Why? Because it was a rocking chair that quietly rocked . . . *on its own.* People who've seen it are convinced they witnessed an unseen spirit slowly rocking back and forth in the old chair.

The mysterious self-rocking chair was in the parlor of the Humphrey House. Visitors have reported peering into the window of the empty parlor and watching the empty chair rock on the old wooden floorboards.

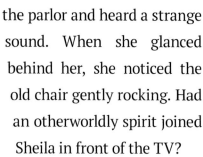

Family member Shelia Humphrey once lived in the house. She remembers when she was watching television by herself in the parlor and heard a strange sound. When she glanced behind her, she noticed the old chair gently rocking. Had an otherworldly spirit joined Sheila in front of the TV?

Donna, whose grandparents once lived in the old house, has also seen the infamous rocking chair move without human intervention. But that pales in comparison to another strange thing she experienced in the home.

Long ago, Donna's grandparents had a butler named Dan Baxter. Dan was a loyal employee who took his job very seriously. He dressed fancily while carrying out his duties, sometimes even wearing a jacket with long coattails and a top hat.

One day, when Donna was eight years old, she was in the kitchen with her grandmother. She looked over and saw Dan, wearing a top hat and holding a serving tray. When she turned away to tell her grandmother about the man in the kitchen, Dan disappeared.

The strange thing about the sighting was that Dan had died many years before Donna spotted him in the kitchen that day!

All of Donna's family members believed her when she told them what she saw, especially her mother.

As Donna got older, she learned most of her family had had experiences with the long dead butler.

Donna's mother had experienced plenty of her own eerie occurrences in the Humphrey House. She'd heard the sounds of movement when there should have been stillness. She'd caught whiffs of strange aromas that disappeared without explanation. And once, while entering a bedroom on the second floor, she'd had a mysterious encounter she could not explain.

That day, as Donna's mother stood in the upstairs bedroom doorway, she'd noticed the room filled with what looked like fog. Puzzled, she looked beyond the room to the window and noticed light suddenly shimmering through the pane of glass. Within moments—before she'd hardly had time to process the strange light—the room cleared, and every trace of the fog vanished.

What did Donna's mother see? Was it the spirit that likes to spend time in the rocking chair? Or was it the dutiful former butler, Dan? Could it have been another spirit yet to introduce itself to the family?

Whoever it was, these odd happenings seem to add up to more than just coincidence.

So, is the old Humphrey House haunted? I suppose it depends on what you believe. But if you ask a Humphrey, chances are they'll convince you that something otherworldly still lingers in the old home.

CHAPTER 7

Eerie Encounters on Water Street

What would you do if you encountered the spirit of a young girl who has not yet crossed over to the other side?

Imagine you are staying over at a relative's home. It is the middle of the night. You are fast asleep in a cozy bed. Suddenly, a soft noise wakes you from your sleep.

You listen carefully, trying to identify the sound, but for a long moment, there's nothing. Only silence.

You decide you must have been dreaming and go back to sleep.

But then . . . you hear it again.

Creak. Creak. Creeeeaaak.

Your eyes open wide. You weren't dreaming at all. As you strain your ears, you can hear it: the sound of soft footsteps. They are walking in the hallway, right outside your bedroom door. A wave of fear rushes over you. You have heard this sound before. You *know* who is pacing the hallway, walking by each of the bedroom doors over and over again.

This late-night walker is not human. At least, not anymore. It is the apparition of a ghostly young girl.

Lucky for you, you're only imagining what you would do in this scenario. But the grandchildren of the people who once owned the Compass Home on North Water Street? They don't have to imagine. They already know. Because it happened to them many times when they slept over at their grandparents' home.

The kids who had this experience in the Compass

House knew they weren't imagining things. Not only could they hear the spirit of the girl walking in the hall, but they could also SEE her! And it wasn't just kids the spirit showed herself to—adults could see her, too.

Everyone who caught a glimpse of the ghostly girl described her in the same way: young, very pale, lovely, and always seen wearing a long, Victorian nightgown.

Those who encountered the spirit could also sense she felt deep sorrow. It seemed as if the ghostly child was grieving—but for whom, or what, remains unknown.

As scary as having a ghost walking outside your bedroom door at night might be, that is not the only frightening thing to happen on the property.

The same kids who saw the ghostly girl made an eerie discovery while rummaging through piles of discarded objects in their grandparents' garden shed. As they dug through boxes and barrels, they found a tombstone!

Brushing off the years of dust, the kids discovered they were holding the tombstone for an infant named

Cyrus Pease Jernigan. The words *"The blighted bud will bloom in heaven"* were carved into the stone, and they sent a chill down the children's spines.

Just who was baby Cyrus, and why was his gravestone in the garden shed at the Compass House? And who is the ghostly girl still lingering in the halls of the historic home? Has Baby Cyrus's death made the girl eternally sad?

Perhaps these mysteries will never be solved.

Or maybe one day they will be. By a curious kid, just like you.

Moshup Beach in Aquinnah

Weird Happenings at Windy Gates

When it was built, Windy Gates estate was the most luxurious home that had ever been built on Martha's Vineyard. Today, it is known as one of the most haunted homes on the island. Lucy Sanford bought the sprawling three-hundred-acre estate in 1891, located just a short distance from the Wequobsque cliffs in Chilmark. As soon as the property was hers, she began to spend lavishly on renovations.

She installed fancy tile imported from Italy and

gold-plated plumbing fixtures into her bathroom. She built stables, constructed a tennis court, and erected a pillared pagoda covered in climbing roses. She even installed electric lights in the pigsty on the property!

The luxurious estate was nothing like the other homes in nearby Chilmark. And those who lived on the property were unlike their rural neighbors. The locals were shocked by the unnecessary and, in their minds, excessive expenditures of Lucy Sanford. They also thought something was very strange about the way Lucy ran her home.

They noticed that the stables she built never

contained horses. No pig ever lived in the well-appointed pigsty. A farmhouse on the property was converted to a groundskeeper's home, but instead of housing a groundskeeper, it was used as a storage area. They gossiped about why Lucy would build so many things, but never use them for their intended purpose.

Islanders thought Lucy Sanford was both extravagant and eccentric—and that opinion never changed.

Very little is known about what happened inside the home. Lucy, a widow, lived on the estate with her daughter, Mary Kobbe, and an employee, Jack Seals.

In time, Mary would wed a mysterious man who claimed to have the royal title of Count.

In the early days of their time in the home, Lucy, Jack, Mary, and her husband threw elaborate parties. But soon, the good times ended.

Mary's husband swindled Lucy, convincing her to make a bad investment on South American railroads. Once she invested a significant portion of her fortune into the Count's scheme, the man disappeared. Soon after he skipped town, the value of the investment crashed, leaving Lucy with little money.

Later, both Mary and Jack died under mysterious circumstances. Lucy kept Mary's and Jack's ashes in urns on the fireplace mantle. Mourning alone in her large home, her mental health suffered. Her daughter was gone. Her fortune was gone. Many say that is when Lucy Sanford lost her mind.

The strange and sad tale of Lucy Sanford ends there, but the legend of her magnificent home remains, along with *plenty* of ghostly tales.

Many have reported seeing the apparition of a

man dressed in stylish clothes from the period when Windy Gates threw its lavish parties. The ghostly figure has been seen on the grounds many times over the years. As unnerving as it might be to spot him, this supposed partygoer from the past is thought to be harmless.

He does not appear to be alone.

Some have spotted a woman dressed in white on the property. This woman sometimes appears to be strolling through the woods or walking through a field. It is only when those who see the woman notice she is actually gliding *several inches above the ground* that they realize it is not a woman at all. It is a ghost!

Still, another ghostly lady has made more than one appearance on the property.

At one time, Roger Baldwin, the man who founded the American Civil Liberties Union in 1920, owned Windy Gates. His family used the estate as a summer home.

Visitors to the historic manor have reported seeing his daughter, Helen, appear on the grounds from beyond the grave. Those who have witnessed her arrival describe it as a show of "heavenly lights," followed by a woman in white dancing.

Perhaps the most bone-chilling of the apparitions reportedly seen on the property is the widow of the Wequobsque Cliffs. This ghost is the reason some describe Windy Gates as "the most notoriously haunted house on Martha's Vineyard."

Supposedly, the otherworldly woman was the wife of a sailor whose whaling ship went missing at sea. To this day, the woman's spirit roams the edge of the cliffs, crying over the loss of her beloved husband. Unable to bear the pain of never seeing him again, the ghostly figure throws herself off the cliff!

This horrible scene has played itself out countless times over the years. Each time, the ghostly woman disappears as she falls into the waves below. But she always returns, again and again, to the place where many believe her life tragically ended.

How many ghosts still linger around Windy Gates? There might be only one way to find out. But who among us is brave enough to go looking for her? Not me!

CHAPTER

9

The Party in the Standish House

Spirits from the Revolutionary War still linger on Martha's Vineyard. One place you can find them is in the Josiah Standish House in West Tisbury. The house was built in 1667. It sits upon Brandy Brow, overlooking Parsonage Pond on State Road.

For many years, the house was known as Whiting Farm. In the 1990s, the five-bedroom home became a bed and breakfast. Once guests started staying at the property and sleeping in the bedrooms, reports of strange happenings began to circulate.

Late one night, a guest needed to use the bathroom, which was in another part of the house. He got out of bed and made his way through the dining room toward the bathroom. As he walked by the living room in his pajamas, he got the shock of his life.

When he peered through the doorway, he saw groups of men dressed in the bright red jackets worn by British soldiers during the Revolutionary War. In the crowd were women wearing the full skirts and bonnets fashionable during colonial times.

The man stared at them all, confused. Had his hosts forgotten to mention a party they were hosting at the inn? A *colonial costume* party? For a few minutes, he stood in the doorway and just watched as the men and women laughed, smoked pipes, and merrily sipped on drinks. *Do some of them have British accents?* he wondered, as he listened in. And their costumes were so authentic looking!

None of the partygoers seemed to notice him, so eventually, the man continued to the bathroom and returned to bed.

The next morning, when he mentioned the party to his hosts, they seemed to have no idea what he was talking about. That is, until he described the men's red coats and the women's colonial dresses. Perhaps there had been a play performed in town? Could this have been a cast party to celebrate their performance?

At that, the innkeeper gave the man a knowing smile. This was not the first time someone had asked this very question in his historic home. He explained that there had been no play and no cast party. Rather, what the man had witnessed was something countless others had *also* seen over the years: the ghostly figures of the notorious British redcoats who had invaded the island many years ago. Even today, the men continue to make use of the inn, dancing and celebrating from beyond the grave.

They were uninvited guests in their lifetime— and remain uninvited almost two and a half centuries later.

A Curious Candle in Oak Bluffs

Just a few blocks inland from Oak Bluffs Town Beach lies a charming old home on Circuit Avenue. Today, the place is known as The Sweet Life Café. But long ago, the wooden building with the lush green yard surrounded by hedges was a family home.

Once, a woman named Joan had a strange experience in the restaurant—and that experience has stayed with her. While dining at the café, Joan believes she might have encountered her grandmother. However, this would be impossible because Joan's grandmother died before Joan was born. Joan's grandmother lived and died in the home on Circuit Avenue and was laid to rest on Martha's Vineyard.

Back in the 1930s, Joan's mother, who was a little girl at the time, and her family lived in the house that is now The Sweet Life Cafe.

Joan's mother loved her own mother very much. Joan never had the chance to meet her mother's mother, her grandmother. Instead, she got to know her grandmother through the stories her mom told her.

Even though Joan never got to meet her grandmother, she still grew up feeling a special connection with her. In fact, every time Joan visits the island where she spent her summers as a child, she visits her grandmother's grave.

Many years after Joan's family moved out of the home, Joan decided to visit the cafe now located in the building. She brought her daughter with her. It was a beautiful and mild spring evening, so Joan and her daughter decided to eat outside in the cafe's garden.

The women were looking forward to their meal. The patio was relaxing and the table setting was charming. Everything was perfect.

Well, almost everything. The candle inside the small hurricane lamp on the table was not lit.

The candles inside the lamps on the tables around them all flickered brightly inside the glass chimneys. The waitress taking care of Joan and her daughter stopped to light the candle on their table. The waitress lit the wick of the candle, but the flame died instantly.

She lit the wick a second time. Once again, she watched the candle begin to burn, and then instantly go out. Puzzled, the waitress took a look at the candle but did not see anything wrong with it. She decided to get them another candle. Perhaps that would solve the problem.

When the waitress returned to Joan's table, she lit the new candle. The women watched as a flame formed on the wick. Within moments, just as before, the flame went out. Again and again, the waitress attempted to light the new candle, but it simply would not stay lit.

It was strange. There appeared to be nothing wrong with *either* of the candles. There was also no breeze that night that would have put out the flame. Every other table in the area glowed with candlelight. What was different at Joan's table?

Despite the problem with the candle, Joan and her daughter had a lovely meal at the café that was once home for Joan's mother and grandmother.

After dinner, the women strolled through the neighborhood, enjoying the lovely spring evening.

Their stroll took them back past the café where they had had dinner. But when they walked by, they noticed something very curious. Every table in the garden, *including* the table where they'd sat, had a lit candle on it.

Joan and her daughter were confused. How could the candle that refused to light so many times while they were at the restaurant be burning brightly now?

Could that have been the unseen spirit of Joan's grandmother trying to communicate? Was she playing games with the candle to welcome them to the place that had once been her home?

If so, it must have *delighted* Joan's grandmother to spend time with her granddaughter and great-granddaughter. Surely, that kind of excitement is worth a blown-out candle or two, isn't it?

CHAPTER 11

The Mighty Moshup

Have you ever heard of Moshup? He is an important part of the culture of the Wampanoag of Noepe. Noepe is name the Wampanoag people used for the island we call Martha's Vineyard today.

Moshup was known as a kind and wise giant. He taught the Wampanoag important skills for survival. He was exceptionally knowledgeable about the sea and whales. He knew so much about whales, he could even transform into one whenever he wanted!

He was also very powerful. He is thought to have

shaped Martha's Vineyard, Nantucket, and other features in Cape Cod.

As the story goes, it was Moshup's massive feet that formed the island. As he walked, his footsteps created enormous imprints into the earth. Some of these imprints filled with ocean water. When the water rushed into Moshup's footprints, the islands and bays of Cape Cod were formed.

Moshup is said to be the reason why the cliffs of Gay Head, now known as Aquinnah, contain red stones. He would wade into the ocean to capture a whale. Then, he would grab the massive mammal by its tail and pluck it from the sea. Finally, he would throw the whale against the rock, killing it. According to legend, the blood from the many whales Moshup caught stained the cliffs with their reddish hue.

The mighty giant shared whales with the Wampanoag. When a whale washed ashore, it was thought to be a gift from Moshup. The giant taught the people how to use each part of the whale, from its meat to its oil and even its bones. The wisdom he shared helped the people survive the harsh conditions on the island, especially in the winters, when it could be extremely cold, snowy, and windy.

At the end of his time with the Wampanoag, Moshup and his wife, Squant, transformed their children into fish and later hid in the cliffs, never to be seen again.

Moshup is not a ghost, but the Wampanoag believe his otherworldly powers aided them in establishing a community on the island. To this day, Moshup is an important part of Wampanoag culture, and his legend continues to be celebrated.

The Vanderhoop House

On the far west side of the island, a gray and white wooden house looms over Rhode Island Sound. Today, it is the Aquinnah Cultural Center, founded to preserve the culture of Aquinnah Wampanoag tribal members.

But one time, long ago, it was a family home.

Edwin Vanderhoop was the man who originally built the structure. He served as Wampanoag's first representative in the Massachusetts legislature in 1888. He constructed the home sometime in the 1890s.

Generations of Vanderhoops lived in the oceanside home. Things were peaceful—until 1928.

It was a sunny December day when four-year-old Elizabeth Vanderhoop went out to play. In her yard was a cistern. A cistern is a large tank used to collect

water. A long time ago, it was common for a house to have a cistern. The tanks held water that people used for drinking and household chores.

In some houses, the cistern was on the roof. When it rained or snowed, water would fill the tank. But the cistern at Elizabeth's house was buried in her yard. The opening of the cistern was covered with an iron manhole cover.

The manhole cover should have been enough to prevent anyone from falling into the water tank.

Unfortunately, the lid of the cistern was broken. When little Elizabeth stepped on the manhole cover, it tilted to the side. She slipped into the tank and fell into four feet of water.

Elizabeth's mother heard the splash and ran outside as fast as she could to rescue her daughter. She lowered a rope into the water tank and urged Elizabeth to grab it. But Elizabeth was so exhausted from trying to keep her head above water, she just could not hang onto the rope.

As the minutes dragged on, the little girl's head slipped beneath the water one final time. Despite her mother's best efforts, Elizabeth drowned in the well.

The death of little Elizabeth was a tragedy. A tragedy so powerful, that many believe the Vanderhoop House is now haunted.

To this day, it is said the grass never grows around the cistern where young Elizabeth took her last breath. But that is not the only strange occurrence that happens in the Vanderhoop home.

Those who have slept in the house have tales to tell. They speak of footsteps coming from seemingly empty hallways. People hear someone walking up and down the staircase when no one is there. Some have even heard the sound of a piano playing on its own, echoing eerily through the vacant house.

Amy Coffey spent four summers in the house. She believes the house is haunted—she has heard the ghostly footsteps herself—but she isn't afraid. "As long as you're respectful of the property and don't change things, you'll be fine. That was how to live there. I felt I had a conversation with a force, an energy, that was there," she said.

Amy also caught a few glimpses of the girl. She once even felt the unseen arms of a ghostly child wrap around her in a comforting hug. Although Amy could not see what was embracing her, she was sure it was a little girl.

"Those people who had less respect for the spirits were haunted more than me," Amy explained.

Another person who spent the summer in the Vanderhoop House recalled seeing the image of

a little girl in the mirror on several occasions. A mysterious little girl has also been spotted in what was once the front yard of the home.

One group of summer roommates recalled a time when they'd all gone to bed with every door locked. When they woke up the next day, however, every door was unlocked! It didn't make any sense— they'd all been asleep and none of them had had any

visitors. Could it have been the spirit of Elizabeth that had unlocked the doors?

Those who've been in the Vanderloop House feel certain spirits dwell within its walls. Does Elizabeth still roam the halls of her former home? And if so, does her spirit roam alone . . . or have *other* ghostly spirits stayed on to keep the little girl company for all eternity?

Something Beneath the Waves

Do you believe in sea monsters? Is it possible there are strange creatures lurking in the ocean that humans have not yet discovered? Have *you* ever seen anything unusual in the water?

Since the beginning of time, there have been legends of sea monsters, dragons, mermaids, and other mysterious creatures that have made the ocean their home. Throughout the ages, sailors have told tales and sang songs of these mystifying monsters who rule the waves and hide in the depths.

But these are just stories, right? Well, maybe not.

Over the years, there have been many reports of sea monsters swimming near Gay Head.

In 1827, Captain Coleman launched his sloop sailboat, *Levant*, and set sail from Nantucket to Connecticut. On that journey, everyone aboard encountered a strange creature in the water. The creature was so bizarre and frightening, it could only be a monster. Or was it?

The captain and others aboard the boat described the creature as sixty feet long, which is about as

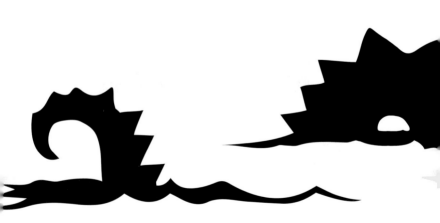

long as a railroad car! The beast reportedly had a barrel-shaped body, a frightening, horselike head, and nostrils that flared as it snorted big gulps of air.

Those aboard later recounted this tale to astonished listeners. They all claimed they'd had a clear view of the creature. It was unlike anything they had ever seen, on land or at sea. The identity of that creature remains a mystery to this day.

That might have been the end of any talk about a monster in the waters near Gay Head, but in 1897, the crew and passengers aboard the steamer *Gloucester*

reported seeing a strange beast swimming off the coast in the same location!

Those aboard the *Gloucester* saw something that looked like a sea serpent. It had a white, eel-like body about six inches in diameter. As it slithered through the water, the crew and passengers thought it looked about forty feet long, which is close to the length of a big school bus. Witnesses noticed the snaky animal had a tapered head and tail. Everyone saw it, but no one had any idea what it was.

The slinking serpent became the talk of the town, and the local newspaper published a story about the sighting. But that extra publicity did not help identify what the creature was. It only caused more people to believe some kind of monster lived in the waters near Gay Head.

In 1930, a sailor navigating his boat near Gay Head also reported seeing something monstrous in the waters. Captain Colwell was aboard his trawler when he spotted a serpentine creature swimming in the waves. Another sea serpent! This creature was yellow. He estimated that the beast was around fifty feet long, about as long as the trailer on an eighteen-wheeler. He said the head of the creature looked like that of a cow.

But that is not all! The captain also said the creature had four small legs. He noticed them when the animal used one of its legs to kick the man's boat out of its way so the pair would not run into each other!

Three sightings of three mysterious creatures in Gay Head. What does it mean? Do sea monsters dwell somewhere off the coast of Gay Head? Or is there a reasonable explanation for all these stories?

Would *you* dare to swim those waters to discover the answer for yourself?

CHAPTER 14

The Sixth Sense

Do you believe in premonitions?

A premonition is a strong feeling that something is about to happen, especially something bad or unpleasant. You may have heard stories of people who decided to delay a trip because something deep inside them told them not to leave at the scheduled time ... only to later discover that the plane or train they would have been on was involved in a terrible accident.

Is that kind of thing a coincidence? Or is there something more to it?

A few well-known islanders have had premonitions that have become part of Martha's Vineyard lore.

Aunt Hillman is one of them.

As a girl, Aunt Hillman was known as Polly Daggett. She was one of the three liberty pole girls. These young women—Polly Daggett, Parnell Manter, and Maria Allen—banded together to work against the British in the Revolutionary War.

In 1778, the British ship *Unicorn* sailed into Vineyard Haven Harbor with a broken spar. The spar on a ship is a pole used to support the ship's sail.

The captain of the ship announced that he would take the town's liberty pole and use it to replace the ship's spar. Liberty poles were used in the colonies to show support for America's independence from

British rule. It would have been an insult for a British ship to take a town's liberty pole by force.

Polly, Parnell, and Maria devised a plan when they heard what the captain intended to do.

Late one night, they crept out to the town's liberty pole. They quietly drilled holes into the pole. Then, they filled those holes with gunpowder and lit a fuse connected to an explosive. The young women ran for cover as the flame reached the gunpowder packed into the pole. Within moments, the gunpowder ignited. The pole exploded into splinters!

Needless to say, the captain did not sail out of the harbor with the town's liberty pole.

Later in life, brave Polly became known for something else. Her psychic powers.

She married a man with the last name Hillman, and soon, the townspeople all called her Aunt Hillman. She was well respected and believed to have otherworldly talents that helped her see into the future.

Aunt Hillman seemed to know about the fate of missing sailors.

In an often repeated story of her skills, she foretold the fate of her brother, Silas Daggett. Silas was a sailor. One day, his ship did not return to the harbor as scheduled. Aunt Hillman knew he would not return to the port alive.

In her mind, she could see her brother. Aunt Hillman somehow knew his body was washed up on some shore. She could see a bruise on her brother's forehead.

Unfortunately, this vision was correct. Her brother's body was later found on a nearby beach. Silas had drowned. When his body was recovered, people couldn't help but notice the sizable bruise on his forehead. It was exactly as Aunt Hillman had foreseen.

How had she known what became of Silas before he

was found? Was this a strange coincidence? Or is this an example of otherworldly abilities?

Aunt Hillman is not the only well-known islander who has shown this strange ability. Buddy Vanderhoop had his own extraordinary experience.

Buddy is a Wampanoag man proud of his heritage. To honor his ancestors, he has worked to make sure the remains of his people have had a respectful final resting place.

One night, Buddy was sailing back from New Bedford, Massachusetts. He had gone there to visit the Peabody Museum. The museum had the skeletal remains of a Wampanoag woman and her two infant daughters. Buddy was there to collect the remains and take them back to the island that had been their home in life.

The evening was dark and foggy. The sky was starless. Even the moon could not peek through the heavy clouds that night. Yet, Buddy was not scared. He had spent his life sailing in the area. Though his boat did not have a searchlight or radar, he knew the way home so well, he wasn't worried about not getting back to the harbor safely.

As Buddy sailed through the fog, he had many thoughts. He felt proud to have the opportunity to bring the mother and her children home. He felt proud of his Wampanoag heritage. He was glad that he could help his ancestors finally rest peacefully.

Despite his calm, however, things quickly changed. Buddy did not understand why, but he

suddenly was struck with the sense that something was wrong. He did not know what it was. He could not see anything through the fog.

Buddy slowed the boat to investigate. Everything looked fine. Nothing seemed to have changed, so why did he have the sense that something bad was about to happen?

It did not take Buddy long to discover the problem.

In the heavy fog, Buddy could not see the huge ocean freighter that was sailing nearby. Thanks

to his strange premonition, he'd stopped his boat to investigate at just the right moment. If he had motored any farther, his boat would have been struck by the massive ship, taking Buddy and his boat to the bottom of the ocean.

Buddy was stunned as he watched the freighter pass in front of his boat. Shaken, he tried to understand what had happened. He concluded that it was his ancestors protecting him on this important journey. He believes the spirits of those he was bringing back to the island guided him that night.

So, what do you think? Are premonitions real? Can the spirits of the dead communicate with the living? Are these stories evidence of otherworldly connections? Those who tell stories of islanders who lived through these events certainly think premonitions are real.

The next time you feel strongly that something is about to happen—maybe a twinge in the pit of your stomach or the urge to do something you cannot explain—ask yourself if someone from beyond the grave could be trying to send you a message.

That is, if you DARE to consider this spine-tingling possibility!

A Ghostly Goodbye

If you've made it this far, you must be pretty brave! You've encountered haunted houses, ghostly children, spooky schools, and other eerie tales—but you kept on reading!

Now that you know the haunted history of Martha's Vineyard, what do you think? Are ghosts real? Is the island REALLY haunted? From Wampanoag folklore and ghostly redcoats, to wailing widows and serpentine sea monsters, there are certainly *many* mysteries to investigate on the Vineyard.

Just one more thing: If you decide to go exploring in hopes of having your own ghostly encounter, watch out! You might get more than you bargained for. Ghosts that seem a little creepy in the book just might be TERRIFYING in real life!

Be sure to stick to places you are allowed to enter. Many people do not welcome ghost hunters on their property. If you get permission to seek out the spirits, make sure your ghostly adventure is a safe one. Remember to stay in groups, take notes, and always watch your back.

After all, you never know who—or *what*—might be right behind you!

Anna Lardinois tingles the spines of Milwaukee locals and visitors through her haunted, historical walking tours known as Gothic Milwaukee. The former English teacher is an ardent collector of stories, an avid walker, and a sweet-treat enthusiast. She happily resides in a historic home in Milwaukee that, at this time, does not appear to be haunted. To learn more, visit annalardinois.com.

Check out some of the other *Spooky America* titles available now!

Spooky America was adapted from the creeptastic *Haunted America* series for adults. *Haunted America* explores historical haunts in cities and regions across America. Here's more from the original *Ghosts of Martha's Vineyard* author Thomas Dresser:

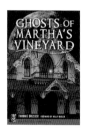
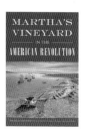

www.thomasdresser.com